Enjoy! Sign your name
after mine + pass it on.

Margaret

Gwen

Sissy

a special gift

presented to:

_____

from:

_____

date:

_____

Sayings, Scriptures, and Stories from
the Bible Revealing God's Love

hugs
from
Heaven

On Angel Wings

G. A. Myers

HOWARD
PUBLISHING CO.

Our purpose at Howard Publishing is to:

- *Increase faith* in the hearts of growing Christians
- *Inspire holiness* in the lives of believers
- *Instill hope* in the hearts of struggling people everywhere

Because He's coming again!

Hugs from Heaven, On Angel Wings
© 1998 by G. A. Myers
All rights reserved. Printed in the United States of America

Published by Howard Publishing Co., Inc.
3117 North 7th Street, West Monroe, LA 71291-2227

02 03 04 05 06 07   10 9 8

Paraphrased Scriptures by LeAnn Weiss, owner of Encouragement Company, 3006 Brandywine Dr., Orlando, FL 32806

Interior Design by LinDee Loveland
Illustrated by Liz Bonham
Edited by Philis Boultinghouse and Janet Reed

Library of Congress Cataloging-in-Publication Data
Myers, G. A., 1955-
    Hugs from heaven on angel wings : sayings, scriptures, and stories
from the Bible revealing God's love / G.A. Myers ; personalized
scriptures by LeAnn Weiss.
        p. cm.
    ISBN 1-878990-90-X
    1. Angels—Biblical teaching. 2. God—Love—Biblical teaching.
3. Bible stories, English—N.T. I. Weiss, LeAnn. II. Title.
BS680.A48M95 1998
235'.3—dc21   98-36851
                                                                                    CIP

Scripture quotations used in this book are from The Holy Bible, New International Version (NIV). Copyright © 1973, 1978, 1984. International Bible Society. Used by permission of Zondervan
Publishing House.

contents

v

Introduction

The *Hugs from Heaven Series* is written with one purpose in mind: to make God's love more real and refreshing to your heart and spirit than ever before. The book is divided into topical sections consisting of a paraphrased scripture, an inspirational message, a poignant saying, and a fictional story based on a particular passage of scripture. Even though the narrative is fictional and the writer takes a creative course with the story, the biblical truths are uncompromised. Favorite Bible stories take on new meaning as you are transported to the scene to explore the thoughts and feelings of the men and women who were touched by heaven's embrace in a special way. May the message in this book, and all of the *Hugs from Heaven* books, bring honor to our God and praise to the Savior, Jesus Christ.

Do not be afraid, Mary

God. You will be with

and you are to give him

great and will be called

The Lord God will give

David, and he will reign o

his kingdom will never

Mary asked the angel,

angel answered, "The

you, and the power of

shadow you. So the holy

the Son of God. Even Eliz

have a child in her old ag

barren is in her sixth mon

with God." "I am

one

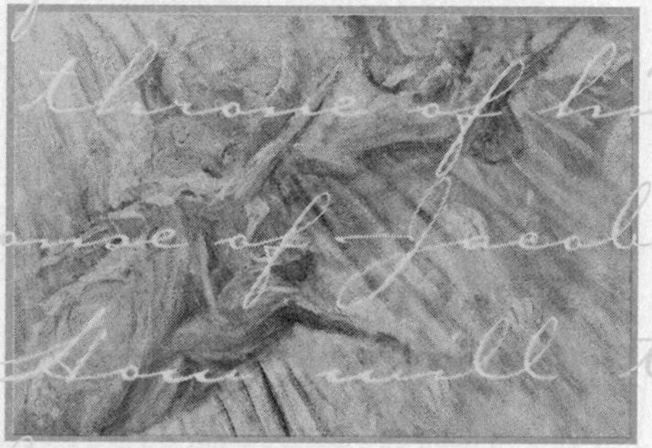

Messengers of Good News

You are cherished and precious in my sight. I've chosen you! You are a royal priest, holy and belonging to me. Declare my praises! I've called you out of darkness into my wonderful light. You are my workmanship, created in Christ Jesus to do good works, which I've already prepared for you to do! I'm working in you to will and to act according to my good purpose for your life.

Your Glorious Father

—from 1 Peter 2:9; Ephesians 2:10; Philippians 2:13

One of the hardest lessons we have to learn in this life . . . is to see the divine, the celestial, the pure in common, the near at hand—to see that heaven lies about us here in this world.

—John Burroughs

Inspirationa

Chosen. The word can bring either feelings of exhilaration or defeat, anticipation or fear. Those fortunate enough to have been gifted with dazzling beauty, amazing athletic ability, or tremendous talent frequently know the excitement of being chosen. They're chosen as special dates, as participants of winning teams, or as main characters in plays. Others, not so blessed in these physical ways, know well the deflating feeling of rejection when they're cut from a team or when they sit by a phone that just doesn't ring. You yourself may have felt the sting of tears after hearing that you weren't quite up to fulfilling that vital purpose or starring in the role you hungered to play. You also may know the sense of pride and fulfillment that comes from being a chosen one.

No matter who we are, we ache to be chosen, because being chosen somehow validates our existence. It means we matter, that we're noticed and appreciated. Above all, it means that someone believes in us.

Hear God's message of good news: Someone *does* believe in you. And that Someone has chosen you—not

Message

because of your beauty or talent but because of his limitless love. This is no ordinary Someone; this is the Lord of lords, the King of kings. He has spent the last two thousand years with your name on his lips and in his heart. He has reached across time to place his nail-scarred hand on your shoulder and say, "I have chosen you."

And now, you are his. You have been chosen to accomplish something very special, something with eternal implications, something that matches the gifts he has given you. Perhaps you've been chosen to parent a child who will ultimately bring peace to our world. Or maybe your task is simply to dry the eyes and heal the hurting heart of a friend. It could be that you've been chosen to share a meal with a hungry person who has a thirsty soul, to be a deeply devoted spouse in a world without loyalties, or to encourage fellow employees when naked cynicism is the standard expression. When circumstances in your life make you feel unwanted or unimportant, just remember— you are chosen. Chosen by love and gifted by grace, you will soon see the one who chose you face to face.

Chosen by Heaven

H

He had been on alert for days. He was becoming restless, wondering not only when he would be called into action, but what his crucially important mission would entail. The archangel Gabriel had experienced every major battle between heaven and earth since the beginning of time. He had witnessed the disheartening and devastating fall of his one-time leader, Lucifer, and the

archangels who had decided to follow, many of whom
had served the Father alongside Gabriel. He knew only
that the message he would soon carry to earth would put
into motion the event on which all history would
hinge. The weight of its importance impassioned him as
nothing had before. Questions ran through his mind:
*Where on earth will I be sent with my message? Whom has
the Father chosen to receive it? Will I face fierce opposition
as I did on my way to minister to Daniel, or is Lucifer still
blindly looking for the key to the Father's plan?*

Finally, the orders arrived. They came from the
Father and were delivered by Michael, who smiled with
excitement as he told Gabriel of his destination. "You
are to deliver a message of good news from the Father.
Go to Nazareth, a town in Galilee, to a virgin pledged
to be married to a man named Joseph, a descendant of
David. The virgin's name is Mary. You may face opposition, so be prepared. This is the time we have all been
waiting for, my friend." Several angels who had accom-

panied Michael embraced Gabriel, one by one. As they shared in the excitement and anticipation, they said to one another, "May the Father's will be done."

On his way to Nazareth, Gabriel had found himself wondering what kind of woman this Mary would be. As he walked the streets of Nazareth's poorest districts, he couldn't help feeling surprised: From this small, unimpressive town would come the hope for humankind. It made him all the more eager to meet the woman the Father had chosen to bring the Messiah into the world. As he neared her home, his excitement grew.

Invisibly, Gabriel slipped into Mary's home and found the chosen one in her room. Gabriel had to smile as he watched her move energetically across the room and say to herself, "Soon I will be wed to the most wonderful man in all of Israel. God has been so good to me." Because of the enormity of the responsibility God was about to place on this woman, Gabriel had thought Mary would be much older. But she was just a young girl.

Gabriel's curiosity grew. What was it about this young girl that made her so special? Of all the women on earth, why had God chosen her? As Gabriel was puzzling over his questions, Mary knelt on the floor. Curious as to what she would do next, Gabriel moved in closer. Mary bowed her head reverently, clasped her hands before her chest, and began to pray.

"Almighty God, I seek you with all my heart. In my poverty you have made me rich; in my times of fear you have given me courage; in my pain you have soothed my heart; in my youth you have made me content." Intensely moved by the depth of her prayer, Gabriel placed his hand gently on her shoulder. To his surprise, Mary turned her cheek as if to nuzzle his hand. She concluded her prayer, "I ask nothing more than to serve you all the days of my life, for my life is worth nothing if not lived to your glory."

Gabriel was stunned. He had not heard such heartfelt words for at least three generations. The prayers of most had become nothing more than rote phrases and trite requests.

Still unseen, Gabriel moved closer to her and searched her face. Her dark eyes were full of excitement. Her olive skin was unblemished and soft. Her black hair, though covered, was thick and long. But most of all he saw that this girl possessed a holy heart, one of immense devotion, a heart that could be trusted with the news he was about to reveal.

Gabriel knew enough of the Father's plan to realize that this innocent, spiritually-minded girl was about to hear the most wonderful news history would ever record. He also knew that in time she would be wounded by the deepest pain a mother could experience. Gabriel felt his face tighten and his arms flex. In a voice she could not hear, Gabriel whispered, "Your unspeakable joy will be matched by unimaginable sorrow. May God bless you, my child. It is easy to understand why the Father has chosen you."

Gabriel arose and made himself visible. Shocked, Mary stood and stepped away from Gabriel as he said, "Greetings, you who are highly favored! The Lord is with you." He wanted to cradle and soothe the startled girl as he shared his news, but he knew any such movement on his part would frighten her even more. "Do not be afraid, Mary," Gabriel said. "You have found favor with God. You will be with child and give birth to a son, and you are to give him the name Jesus. He will be great and will be called the Son of the Most High. The Lord God will give him the throne of his father David, and he will reign over the house of Jacob forever; his kingdom will never end."

As the news settled into Mary's heart, her expression turned to one of puzzlement, and she asked, "How will this be since I am a virgin?"

Gabriel moved closer, and she felt his warm touch on her shoulder. "The Holy Spirit will come upon you, and the power of the Most High will overshadow you.

So the holy one to be born will be called the Son of God. Even Elizabeth your relative is going to have a child in her old age, and she who was said to be barren is in her sixth ‚month." Then Gabriel, inspired by the magnitude of the unfolding events, proclaimed what every angel knows and Mary would soon learn. "For nothing is impossible with God."

Regaining her composure, Mary lifted her head and looked into Gabriel's kind eyes and said, "I am the Lord's servant. May it be to me as you have said." With that, Gabriel left her, rejoicing as he made his way to his heavenly dwelling.

Gabriel knew he would never forget his visit with the virgin through whom God would visit the world.

Scriptural Account

In the sixth month, God sent the angel Gabriel to Nazareth, a town in Galilee, to a virgin pledged to be married to a man named Joseph, a descendant of David. The virgin's name was Mary. The angel went to her and said, "Greetings, you who are highly favored! The Lord is with you."

Mary was greatly troubled at his words and wondered what kind of greeting this might be. But the angel said to her, "Do not be afraid, Mary, you have found favor with God. You will be with child and give birth to a son, and you are to give him the name Jesus. He will be great and will be called the Son of the Most High. The Lord God will give him the throne of his father David, and he will reign over the house of Jacob for ever; his kingdom will never end."

"How will this be," Mary asked the angel, "since I am a virgin?"

The angel answered, "The Holy Spirit will come upon you, and the power of the Most High will overshadow you. So the holy one to be born will be called the Son of God. Even Elizabeth your relative is going to have a child in her old age, and she who was said to be barren is in her sixth month. For nothing is impossible with God."

"I am the Lord's servant," Mary answered. *"May it be to me as you have said." Then the angel left her.*

—Luke 1:26–38

Moments I have felt heaven's tender embrace . . .

_____

_____

_____

_____

_____

_____

_____

_____

_____

_____

_____

_____

_____

_____

_____

_____

I have redeemed you! You've been purposely chosen by me.
You are mine.

—from Isaiah 43:1

_____

_____

_____

_____

_____

_____

_____

_____

_____

_____

_____

_____

_____

_____

You are my workmanship, created in Christ Jesus to do good works which I've already prepared you in advance to do!

—from Ephesians 2:10

Suddenly a great comp

appeared with the ange

"Glory to God in the h

ven on whom his favor

left them and gone into t

one another, "Let's go to B

that has happened, whic

So they hurried off and f

the baby, who was lyin

had seen him, they spre

had been told them abo

heard it were amazed at

them. But Mary treas

pondered them in her he

glorifying and praising

two

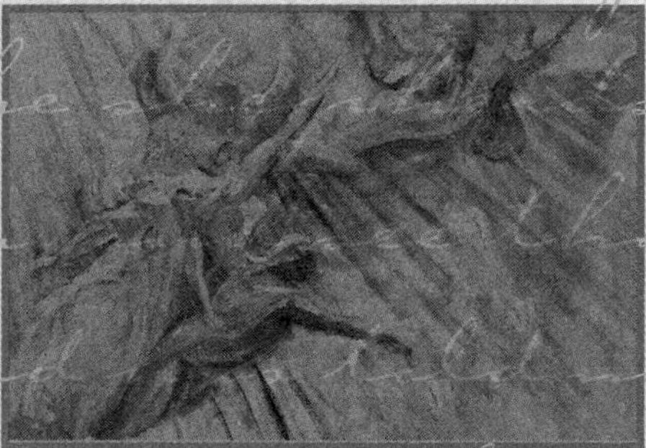

Messengers of Joy

Look for and remember my holy moments.
I've made my light shine in your heart to give
you the knowledge of my glory in the face of
Christ. I've given you this treasure in jars of
clay to remind you that this all-surpassing
power is from me and not from you.

Your Holy God

—from 2 Corinthians 4:6–7

Angels are unsatisfiable in their longing to do by all means all manner of good unto all the creatures . . . especially the children of men.

—Richard Hooker

Inspirational

You may not know it, but you have in your possession treasures of immeasurable worth. You didn't buy them with a check or credit card—you couldn't have afforded them if you'd tried, and they're not for sale if you could. Even though they are more precious than all the possessions you've accumulated throughout your whole life, you may be allowing them to gather dust in a dark corner of your mind. These treasures were given to you as a gift, a blessing, and if you look with spiritual eyes, you'll see them as explosions of brilliant color on the canvas of your life.

I speak of holy moments, experiences you have witnessed or participated in that were so rich with meaning that your life would be dull and destitute without them. Perhaps one such moment was an act of kindness that led to a lifelong friendship, a date

Message

that led to matrimony, or a kiss on the cheek of a precious infant. Maybe you've experienced the brush of a tiny, inquisitive hand against your own or a view of God's creation that affirmed a wavering faith. Possibly a message of joy was delivered to your heart on a lonely night from the loving God who knew you needed assurance.

Whatever holy moments you've experienced, now is the time to throw open the windows of your mind and allow the light to shine on those vibrant moments. Pour a cup of coffee and find the photo album. Sit on the porch with someone special and open the door to the storage closet of your mind. Wipe the dust from their memory, polish them up, and let the beauty and wonder of heaven's gifts impact your today, tomorrow, and the rest of your life.

Silent Night

The absolute silence echoed in Hallel's ears. No one spoke a word; not a wing fluttered. Even more amazing, the sound of praise and worship that continually echoed through the halls of heaven had ceased. The angel could not remember another time like it: Heaven was silent. Hallel would never have believed there would be a time when he was not leading a heavenly host in a vast assortment of songs and choruses. As the angel of praise, he was ordained to lead heaven in perpetual adulation and ceaseless song, and he carried out his duties joyfully.

The Father had gifted him with a clear, inviting voice, which emboldened even the most timid angel to join the worship with wholehearted enthusiasm, and his face beamed with a constant smile. Even in this uncommon and rather uncomfortable silence, his eyes blazed with anticipation, as he thought about the sequence of events that had led to this moment and the miracle that was about to unfold. All of heaven and earth had looked forward to the coming occurrence since the Father had formed humans in his image.

Hallel had been preparing songs of praise for the anticipated event when Gabriel had delivered the unsettling message. If the request had not come directly from Gabriel, Hallel would have thought it a deception from Lucifer or one of his cohorts. But the excitement in Gabriel's voice and the urgent expression on his face punctuated his plea with authenticity. Gabriel instructed him to leave his perch of praise and fly immediately to the throne room of Almighty God.

Putting Micah, his assistant, in charge of the heavenly chorus, Hallel flew to his meeting with lightning speed. He entered the glorious presence of the Father and covered his face with his wings as he knelt before God, saying, "Glory be to you, Almighty Father. How may I serve you?"

With a voice as beautiful as a comforting wind, the Father spoke, "Hallel, you have served me well, from the beginning until now. Your brilliant songs of praise have been heard from the depths of the earth to the farthest reaches of the heavenlies. I know you may be confused by my instructions; however, I am confident you will carry them out as I ask, for you follow me out of love.

"Very soon, the most wonderful incident of all measured time will take place on earth. You know the event I speak of?"

"Yes, my Lord, I was preparing praises for the birth when you called."

With a broad smile, the Father continued. "Gather your heavenly host and prepare to go where my Son will be born. You are to arrive in Bethlehem on the day of the birth. But when you get there, do not make a sound: no songs, no praise, no speech. You are to be completely silent."

A baffled look swept Hallel's face. His wings trembled. "No songs of worship?" he asked. The Father affirmed, "None."

"But Father," Hallel boldly protested, "I find it difficult to refrain from breaking into praise just being in your presence this short time. How can I keep the whole host, let alone myself, quiet in anticipation of your Son's birth?"

The Father's eyes brightened even more, "Hallel, my Son's birth will be a holy occurrence that will never be repeated. The future of the world revolves around the birth of my Son. Hearts will be healed, the dead will be raised, fear will be defeated, and my enemy Satan will no longer be able to steal the joy of my children. Love that has grown stale will be renewed, fullness will replace emptiness, and dreams will become reality. In honor of this sacred moment, the night shall be silent when my Son enters the world. Go in silence and witness this sacred event with the heavenly host nearby. When you hear the first cry from the lips of the infant and see the first quiver of his lips, gather your host and deliver the message of joy that the Savior is born."

Immediately Hallel asked, "Who shall receive this wonderful announcement? Which king or ruler?"

"No dignitary is worthy of this news. Go to the faithful, the poor, and the weak. Go first to the shepherds outside the city of Bethlehem who raise my sacrificial lambs. They shall hear the news first because my Son will be both sheep and shepherd for my people." As the Father spoke, he held out a book. "When you make the announcement, sing this song. Sing it so that it fills heaven and earth and the caverns of hell with the announcement that victory belongs to the Father and his children."

Hallel looked at the book, smiled with appreciation, and turned, saying, "Your will be done, my Lord and my God."

Hallel immediately gathered his host from their stations across the heavens, and they sang as they made their way to the little town of Bethlehem. Since the setting of earth's sun until now, not a word had been uttered by any heavenly being, and the night was silent as never before. As the host waited in the distance, Hallel posted himself in the stable with Mary and Joseph, awaiting his signal. Unseen, he paced back and forth with Joseph. Hallel winced at the virgin's birth pains, prayed for her relief, and stared in amazement at the first sight of the child's head. As Joseph spoke words of encouragement to Mary, Hallel found himself cheering her on as well, "That's it, Mary. You can do it. Just a little longer."

Then Hallel heard it: the soft cry that was quickly quieted at Mary's breast. Hallel sprang up, flexed his mighty wings, and flew to the waiting host. He wanted to shout for joy to the whole world, but he knew the first words were for the shepherds. He waved to the host to follow him to the nearby fields. There he found the chosen shepherds tending their sheep. He watched for a moment and thought to himself, *These shepherds have no idea that their lives are about to be changed forever.* Instantly he appeared to them in a flash of glory. The shepherds ran backwards in fear, but Hallel approached them, glowing with delight. "Do not be afraid. I bring you good news of great joy that will be for all the people." As he spoke, they cautiously moved closer, drawn by his warm smile and inviting voice. "Today in the town of David a Savior has been born to you; he is Christ the Lord." The shepherds knelt at the sound of the news. "This will be a sign to you: You will find a baby wrapped in cloths and lying in a manger." Hallel turned and commanded, "Sing the song the Lord has given us," and the heavenly host appeared and filled the silent night with praise. Hallel joined the throng and together they sang, "Glory to God in the highest, and on earth peace to men on whom his favor rests." They sang it again and again, louder with each refrain. The shepherds joined the singing with all their hearts and danced around the flock. As the host retreated, the song hung in the air, a sweet incense of praise.

Hallel followed the shepherds into the town where they found the Savior, just as he had told them. As they knelt in wonder, he knelt invisibly with them, placed his wings around them, and quietly sang again,

"Glory to God in the highest, and on earth peace to men on whom his favor rests."

Scriptural Account

And there were shepherds living out in the fields near by, keeping watch over their flocks at night. An angel of the Lord appeared to them, and the glory of the Lord shone around them, and they were terrified. But the angel said to them, "Do not be afraid. I bring you good news of great joy that will be for all the people. Today in the town of David a Savior has been born to you; he is Christ the Lord. This will be a sign to you: You will find a baby wrapped in cloths and lying in a manger."

Suddenly a great company of the heavenly host appeared with the angel, praising God and saying, "Glory to God in the highest, and on earth peace to men on whom his favor rests."

When the angels had left them and gone into heaven, the shepherds said to one another, "Let's go to Bethlehem and

Messengers of Joy

see this thing that has happened, which the Lord has told us about."

So they hurried off and found Mary and Joseph, and the baby, who was lying in the manger. When they had seen him, they spread the word concerning what had been told them about this child, and all who heard it were amazed at what the shepherds said to them. But Mary treasured up all these things and pondered them in her heart. The shepherds returned, glorifying and praising God for all the things they had heard and seen, which were just as they had been told.

—Luke 2:8–20

Moments I have felt heaven's tender embrace . . .

_____
_____
_____
_____
_____
_____
_____
_____
_____
_____
_____
_____
_____
_____
_____
_____

*I sent my precious Son, Jesus, to you from heaven to shine
on those living in darkness and in the shadow of death.*

—from Luke 1:79

Jesus answered, "It is u

bread alone, but on every

mouth of God.'" Then th

city and had him stand

temple. "If you are the

yourself down. For it is

his angels concerning you,

their hands, so that yo

against a stone.'" Jesus

written: 'Do not put the

Again, the devil took him

showed him all the king

splendor. "All this I w

will bow down and wors

"Away from me, Satan!

three

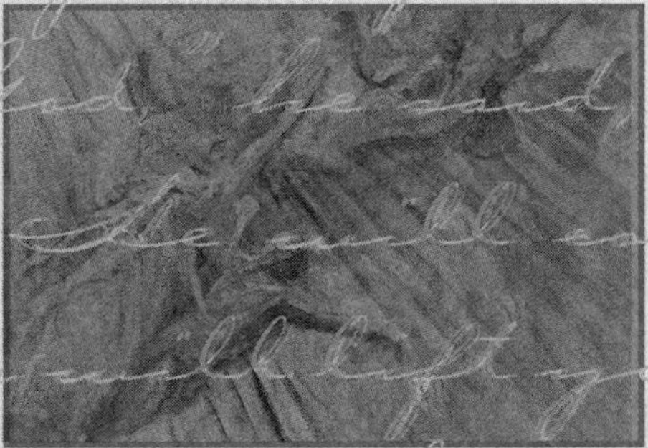

Messengers of Comfort

Don't let circumstances discourage you or make you fearful. Know that you are not alone because I am with you wherever you are. My Word is the antidote for temptation. I am more than able to keep you from falling and to make you stand without fault in the presence of my glory with rejoicing, because all glory, majesty, power, and authority belong to me.

Your Refuge and God Most High

—from Joshua 1:9; 1 Corinthians 10:13; Jude 24–25

S

Sleep, my child, and
peace attend thee
All through the night,
Guardian angels God
will send thee,
All through the night.

—Sir Harold Boulton

Inspirational

There is something you most definitely need to know. It is one of the most compelling of all truths. You may have already learned this truth while enduring hardship or struggling through the stormy torrents of this life. Once you know it, once you really become aware of it in the depths of your heart and soul, you will never again look into the face of evil with fear or walk in darkness feeling lost and abandoned.

Look into a mirror and recite these words to the person you see: *You are not alone.* Say it again and allow the words to blow over you like a refreshing wind. *You are not alone.*

It is a simple message of comfort, but it is heavy with importance. God has eagerly heralded it in his Word since he formed our flesh and breathed life into our lungs. When you feel burdened by life's heaviest

Message

decisions and your knees begin to buckle under the weight, he says, "Come to me." When you hunger because the world's offerings have left you empty, he says, "Eat this bread and drink this cup." When you need encouragement to persevere past the pain of rejection or heartache, he reminds you that you have a great cloud of heavenly witnesses cheering you on. When failure and disappointment become your companions or loneliness threatens your faith, he says, "Never will I leave you, never will I forsake you." When Satan's lies of the Father's desertion make their way through the cracks of your faith, revisit the promise of our loving God: "Draw near to me and I will draw near to you." Move into his open arms as he wraps them around you gently and pulls you close. His smile says it all: *You are never alone.*

Applause from Heaven

The bright colors of the rainbow in the distance presented a stark contrast to the sun-baked earth tones of the desert, especially where the two met on the thin line of the horizon. As the archangel Michael viewed the scene, he felt the same contrast within himself. He sensed the approaching end to the grueling confrontation between his one-time superior and now nemesis,

Lucifer, and the Messiah. He had savored the satisfaction of watching the Messiah defy the evil one's relentless stream of temptations during these nearly forty days. Yet he doubted that the roaring lion had retreated from the hunt.

As Jesus neared the end of his time in the desert he had called home for the last several weeks, he was drained and exhausted. The dual strain of fasting and standing firm against Satan had gravely affected his physical health. In a bare whisper, Jesus said to his Father, "I am so hungry and tired." As Michael watched the Son of Man stumble and nearly fall as his legs buckled beneath him, he asked the Father if he could now go and minister to Jesus. The angel was surprised by the answer. "No, not yet, Michael. The dragon isn't done with this battle, and neither is my Son."

No sooner had the Father finished speaking than Michael heard the familiar deep and raspy voice of Lucifer: "That's right Michael." The evil one hovered near Jesus' weary body as he spoke. "I am far from finished. Everything until now was meant simply to cripple, not to destroy. I am now ready to assault him with my most powerful temptations . . . while he is in his weakest state."

Michael quickly positioned himself between Jesus and Lucifer, saying, "I know well the tactics that caused the fall of Adam, Israel, David, and others. Remember, I was there. The Father's grace defeated you then, and his love for his children will defeat you now. Don't forget that I am nearby, eagerly awaiting the Father's command to move."

Suddenly, Satan made himself visible to Jesus, and his ugly gutteral voice became sweet and soothing. "If you are the Son of God, tell these stones to become bread."

Even though Jesus' weakened body craved to do just as Satan suggested, his whisper-soft voice gained strength with every word as he answered, "It is written:

'Man does not live on bread alone, but on every word that comes from the mouth of God.' " At these words, an echo of cheers could be heard from the heavenlies.

The devil then took Jesus by the hand and led him to the holy city. Michael followed close behind, longing to be told he could move to the Messiah's aid. Satan stood with Jesus on the highest point of the temple and said with intimidating arrogance, "If you are the Son of God, throw yourself down. For it is written: 'He will command his angels concerning you, and they will lift you up in their hands, so that you will not strike your foot against a stone.' " He looked momentarily at Michael and bobbed his head as if to say, "Isn't that true, Michael?"

Jesus answered him with a clear voice, surprising in its strength, "It is also written: 'Do not put the Lord your God to the test.' " Again, as the words left the lips of Jesus, a wall of cheering filled the heavens and Michael smiled.

Next, the devil took Jesus to a high mountain and showed him all the kingdoms of the world and their splendor. With his long, elegant fingers, he pointed out the cities, palaces, and beautiful buildings. Then in a richly sincere voice, he said, "All this I will give you, if you will only bow down and worship me."

As Michael listened attentively to this latest temptation, he thought to himself, *You liar; only you would offer what you do not own.*

Jesus' eyes flashed with life and his back straightened. Without hesitation, he looked into the face of the devil and said, "Away from me, Satan! For it is written: 'Worship the Lord your God, and serve him only.'" The intensity with which Jesus spoke set Satan back on his heels. All traces of his smile vanished, and he covered his ears against the sea of praise and applause the angel host poured down upon the mountain. Suddenly, he turned and disappeared into a cloud of darkness as he spat his threats of return and ultimate victory.

With loud songs of adoration still filling the air like endless rolls of thunder, the Father spoke to Michael, "Quickly, send your angels to attend to my Son's needs." Immediately a score of angels descended and encircled Jesus, offering encouragement, embraces, food, and drink. Comforted and filled, the Messiah lay down to sleep. Michael flew to the sleeping form and placed Jesus' weary head in his lap. As he lovingly brushed his sweaty hair from his face, he said, "Sleep sweetly, O King—both God and man. We are so proud of you. Only heaven witnessed your courage and holiness today, but one day all the world will know of it. The evil one is not through with you yet. You will face him again, but the love of the Father and all of heaven will sustain you."

Scriptural Account

Then Jesus was led by the Spirit into the desert to be tempted by the devil. After fasting forty days and forty nights, he was hungry. The tempter came to him and said, "If you are the Son of God, tell these stones to become bread."

Jesus answered, "It is written: 'Man does not live on bread alone, but on every word that comes from the mouth of God.'"

Then the devil took him to the holy city and had him stand on the highest point of the temple. "If you are the Son of God," he said, "throw yourself down. For it is written: 'He will command his angels concerning you, and they will lift you up in their hands, so that you will not strike your foot against a stone.'"

Jesus answered him, "It is also written: 'Do not put the Lord your God to the test.'"

Again, the devil took him to a very high mountain and showed him all the kingdoms of the world and their splendor. "All this I will give you," he said, "if you will bow down and worship me."

Jesus said to him, "Away from me, Satan! For it is

written: 'Worship the Lord your God, and serve him only.'"

Then the devil left him, and angels came and attended him.

—Matthew 4:1–11

*M*oments I have felt heaven's tender embrace . . .

_____

_____

_____

_____

_____

_____

_____

_____

_____

_____

_____

_____

_____

_____

_____

_____

_____

_____

I am your refuge and your fortress, your God, in whom you trust.

—from Psalm 91:3

Jesus went out as usual
his disciples followed hi
said to them, "Pray that
tation." He withdrew a
them, knelt down and
willing, take this cup fr
yours be done." An angel
and strengthened him.
prayed more earnestly, a
of blood falling to the
prayer and went back to
asleep, exhausted from sor
he asked them. "Get up a
fall into temptation."

four

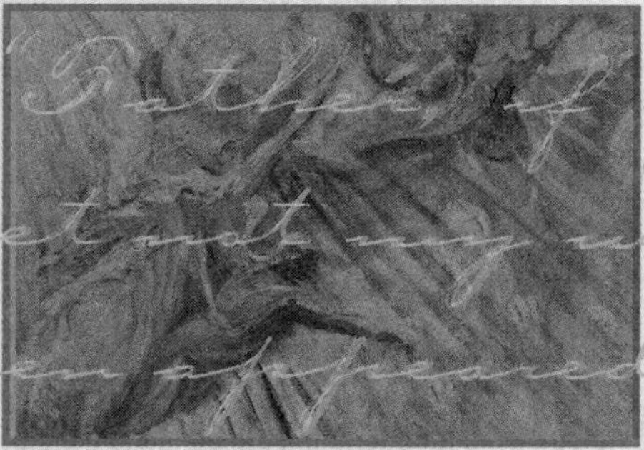

Messengers of Courage

Find rest in me. I am your refuge and your fortress, your God, in whom you trust. You can count on me to save you from the enemy's wearying detours and obstacles. My faithfulness goes before you. You don't have to worry day or night, for I will command my angels concerning you. They'll guard you in all your ways. Because you love me, I will rescue and protect you. When you call upon me, I will answer you. I will be with you in trouble. I will deliver you and honor you. You can do all things because I empower you.

Your God of Strength

—from Psalm 91:1–15; Philippians 4:13

We only live among men, but there are airy hosts, blessed spectators, sympathetic lookers-on, that see and know and appreciate our thoughts and feelings and acts.

—Henry Ward Beecher

Inspirational

Are you tired of running the race of life? Are you carrying more weight on your shoulders than you can safely handle? Are you consumed by a quiet desperation when you think about the future? Do you crave a simpler, more balanced life?

I have some good news for you. My message is not profound, but it will bring a light to your eyes and courage to your heart. Are you ready? You have a Father who loves you deeply. And he is waiting for you at home—your real home, in heaven.

Pretty simple, isn't it? God's Word tells us that thoughts of God's love and home helped Jesus endure the Cross. During his last and most stressful week on earth, he spoke of his Father's house and the many rooms being prepared for you.

Can you picture it? The fresh fragrance of new construction fills the place. The air holds excite-

Message

ment and anticipation. The warm love of the living God illuminates each room and every hallway. No fear lurks in the darkness because there is no darkness there. And listen, do you hear the music? It's the joyful song of the angels. You can't help but join the chorus.

Approach the doorway where Jesus stands. With one nail-scarred hand he points to a golden nameplate and with the other he touches your shoulder. The nameplate bears your name. Hear his gentle voice say, "One day you will be with me in this place, and all that you are going through now will seem as nothing."

Until that day, don't take your eyes off the love of the Father or the place he has prepared for you. Everything else will pass, but your home will stand forever.

By the way, how would you like your room decorated?

Your Blood Will Save the World

They entered the Garden of Gethsemane as darkness chased away dusk's lingering light. Jesus looked at the horizon as the last ember of sunlight disappeared at the fine line that separates earth and sky. His disciples followed close behind, sensing the mysterious sorrow behind the eyes of the magnificent man they had followed these three years. At supper they had listened to

Jesus speak of strange, final things, and now they exchanged quizzical glances, hoping that perhaps one of them had an answer to what it all meant.

John quietly asked, "Do you think it has something to do with what happened with Judas and why he isn't here with us?" His only answer was some scattered shrugs.

"Why do you think he told me I would deny him?" Peter asked with a troubled expression. Then he mumbled to himself, "How could he ask such a question? The Master knows I would never desert him . . . doesn't he?"

Jesus heard them talking and was aware of their confusion and concern. As he neared his favorite place of prayer, he stopped, looked into their faces, and forced a smile. He so wanted to put his arms around them and explain it all in a way they could understand. But how could he? How could any human truly understand the spiritual war that was about to be waged between heaven and hell? Instead he said, "Pray that you will not fall into temptation."

He walked the twenty yards to his special spot and deeply inhaled the gentle wind. It was heavy with moisture. Spring growth fragranced the air with sweetness. How precious this piece of earth had become to him! He had spent countless hours here in communion with the Father. Here, the human and divine met in one body and spoke with one voice to achieve one outcome: the rescue and redemption of the world.

He paused, thinking about what the next twenty-four hours would bring. Then he opened his hands and looked at the palms that had healed and comforted so many. He pressed a finger hard into the center of his right hand and tried to imagine the sensation of heavy metal spikes nailing his hands and feet to wood beams. A shudder ran through his body. His humanity recoiled against the pain he knew he must endure. When he closed his eyes he could hear the venomous insults that would pierce his heart. The angry voices left him cold and clammy. He opened his eyes and turned them toward the night sky and thought of home and Father. Overwhelmed with agony and loneliness, his legs gave way. His knees hit the ground, and he fell forward at the waist. The words spilled from his lips as if pouring from a broken vessel, "Father, if you are willing, take this cup from me." Then quietly . . . slowly, he added, "Yet not my will but yours be done." Great tears of grief fell to the ground, and he hugged his arms against his abdomen as he wept.

The angel Gabriel had been sent to the garden by the Father to stand watch. The Father would send no other, for it was Gabriel who had announced the coming of the Messiah to Mary, and now he would be God's messenger of courage at the end of Christ's life. He was sent to encourage and strengthen Jesus for the brutal experience that would soon begin. Thus far, he had watched and listened from the shadows. Now, he came and knelt beside the suffering Savior. Gently engulfing Jesus with his powerful wings, Gabriel warmed his Lord against the chills that shivered through his body. Jesus lifted his head at the warm embrace from heaven, and the eyes of heaven met the eyes of earth.

Locking his eyes on those of his Master, Gabriel said, "I have a message from the Father. These are his exact words: 'If I could remove you from this place and still save these people we love so deeply, you know I would. If I could wash away the sins of the world without your blood, I would not hesitate to end your agony. And even now, my Son, you know that if you say the word, the angel I have sent will call out and I will destroy all those who want to harm you. But I know you will not. Be strong and courageous, my Son. After you have suffered a little while, I will welcome you home.'"

Gabriel cradled Jesus in his arms. Being in anguish, Jesus prayed even more earnestly. His sweat fell like drops of blood to the ground. When he rose from prayer, Jesus knew the time had come. Gabriel put his strong hands on Jesus' shoulders, spread his wings wide, and placed his forehead against the Savior's. Looking into Jesus' eyes, Gabriel repeated three times, "The Father loves you; your blood will save the world."

When Jesus walked back to the disciples, he found them asleep. "Why are you sleeping?" he asked as he wakened them. "Get up and pray so that you will not fall into temptation."

Gabriel was filled with sadness as he watched the approaching crowd, led by Judas the betrayer, surround Jesus. As Judas leaned forward with a kiss of greeting for Jesus, Gabriel repeated to himself, "The Father loves you; your blood will save the world."

Scriptural Account

Jesus went out as usual to the Mount of Olives, and his disciples followed him. On reaching the place, he said to them, "Pray that you will not fall into temptation." He withdrew about a stone's throw beyond them, knelt down and prayed, "Father, if you are willing, take this cup from me; yet not my will, but yours be done." An angel from heaven appeared to him and strengthened him. And being in anguish, he prayed more earnestly, and his sweat was like drops of blood falling to the ground.

When he rose from prayer and went back to the disciples, he found them asleep, exhausted from sorrow. "Why are you sleeping?" he asked them. "Get up and pray so that you will not fall into temptation."

—Luke 22:39–46

Moments I have felt heaven's tender embrace . . .

_____

_____

_____

_____

_____

_____

_____

_____

_____

_____

_____

_____

_____

_____

_____

_____

When you earnestly seek me with all of your heart, I promise you will find me.

—from Jeremiah 29:13

_____

_____

_____

_____

_____

_____

_____

_____

_____

_____

_____

_____

_____

_____

_____

_____

I won't play hide-and-seek with you. As you draw near to me, watch me come close to you.

—from James 4:8

There was a violent eart[h]

Lord came down from he[aven]

rolled back the stone and

was like lightning, and

snow. The guards were

shook and became like dea[d]

women, "Do not be afraid, f[or]

ing for Jesus, who was cr[ucified]

risen, just as he said. Com[e]

lay. Then go quickly and

risen from the dead and

Galilee. There you will

you." So the women hu[rried]

afraid yet filled with j[oy]

ples. Suddenly Jesus me[t]

five

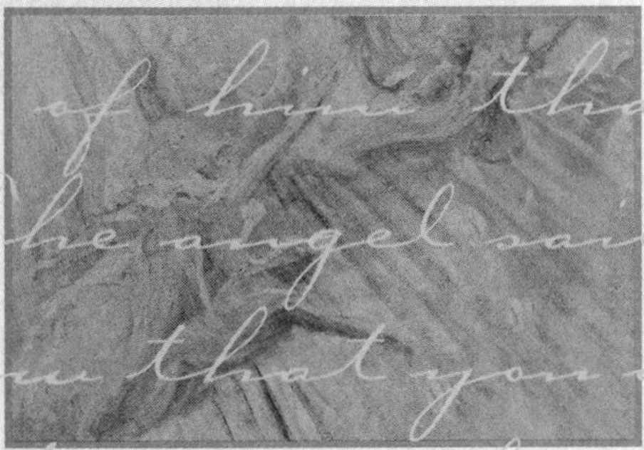

Messengers of Blessing

Because of my extravagant mercy, I've given you a new birth into a living hope through the resurrection of Jesus Christ from the dead. In this world you will have trouble and disappointments. The good news is that you can take heart because I have already overcome the world. I am near to the brokenhearted and the crushed in spirit. When you eagerly seek me with all of your heart, you'll find me.

Your Near God

—from 1 Peter 1:3; John 16:33; Psalm 34:18; Jeremiah 29:13

Millions of spiritual creatures walk the earth unseen, both when we wake and when we sleep.

—John Milton

Inspirational

If your life is basically trouble free, conflicts nonexistent, failures too few to mention, and disappointments seldom darken your door, you can skip right past this message. However, if you are like the rest of us, and it seems that every day presents some new dilemma, failures accumulate with age, and disappointments overshadow the starry-eyed dreams of youth, remember: *God blesses those who earnestly seek him.*

This promise glows like a beacon in our future and acts as a cleansing shower to our past. It plainly states that God blesses our simple faith. He does not measure your looks, accomplishments, wealth, or deeds before opening his arms and touching your life. He doesn't tally your missteps, poor choices, or self-inflicted troubles before releasing his blessings. He wants only for

Message

you to want him, to pursue him, to step with a believing heart into his strong embrace. He will revive dead dreams and give birth to new vision.

Allow the hope of this promise to work into your wounds, cuts, and bruises like a soothing salve. Look at the kind of people who have already received this promise: The stumbling Peter walked on water and was honored to open the gates of heaven with the keys of the kingdom. A despised tax collector ate supper with a divine Savior and found salvation. Poor peasants were parents to the King of kings. Deserting disciples turned the world upside down. Two Marys, armed with spices to cover the stench of death, were the first to find that failed hopes and dreams were alive. Good news? The best you will ever hear. You will never be disappointed while seeking God.

The Weeping Marys

Early Sunday morning, the sun crept slowly across the room, as if looking for someone to awaken. When it reached Mary's bed, it discovered her fully awake, her eyes swollen from hours of uncontrollable weeping. All night long, violent emotions had shaken her body and then erupted in tears. Each eruption was followed by a series of trembling sighs as she tried to regain her composure. But the reprieve lasted only a few moments before she would be hit by another quake, and the whole process would begin again. Her entire body ached from the ordeal. The sunlight forced her awareness of the new day, and a sweet fragrance of freshly fallen rain graced her red nose. She took a deep breath, trying to ease her crying.

Mary Magdalene had never felt such agonizing sorrow. Not even her years of prostitution had produced the loneliness and heartache she now felt. All she had to do was whisper his name, and the whole scene—beating, insults, crucifixion—leaped fresh to her mind. Sleep had come in short snatches, and even then she dreamed of the crowd's relentless call for Christ's crucifixion. She had spent the Sabbath tearfully repeating unanswered questions: Why did they hate him so much? What did he ever do but love everyone he met—even a stained prostitute? She lifted her head and directed her questions heavenward: "O God, why did they kill my hope, my dreams, my life? I wish now I had died *with* him rather than face life *without* him." Her body heaved with the pain and tears sprang to her eyes once again.

Through her sobs she heard a voice: "Mary! Mary! Are you awake?" Recognizing the voice of her friend, Mary the mother of James, Mary Magdalene opened the door, and the two women fell into each other's arms. Muffling their wails so as not to disturb sleeping neighbors, the women comforted each other. Finally, Mary Magdalene pulled away and said, "Before we go to the tomb, let us pray the prayer Jesus taught us. Maybe it will ease our pain, if only for a few moments."

The two weeping women knelt together and prayed, "Our Father in heaven, hallowed be your name." When Mary Magdalene's voice faltered, the other Mary continued alone, "Your kingdom come, your will be done, on earth as it is in heaven . . ."

When they finished the Lord's prayer, Mary the

mother of James concluded, "And please let us know that everything will somehow be all right. Amen." Little did they know just how clearly their words were heard in heaven.

The angel Azeal was poised and ready. Michael and Gabriel had been given the order to move the stone away from the tomb, and every heavenly being eagerly awaited word that Christ had risen. Joyful preparations had been made for the return of the Son to his place at the right hand of the Father. Summoned to the throne of the Most High, Azeal approached the Father and knelt before him. "Almighty," he said, "your servant awaits your command."

"Azeal, I have been touched by the prayers and petitions of two faithful servants who followed my Son to the Cross. They have chosen to visit the tomb this morning, but they will not understand what they will find there. Follow them to the grave, see that they are safe, and give them this message for me: 'He is not here; he has risen, just as he said.' Tell them they will see him again, and comfort them, for they are fretful and frightened."

As bidden, Azeal flew to join the two Marys. The weeping women gathered the spices they had prepared for Jesus' body, shut the door to Mary Magdalene's home, and began the slow walk to the tomb where Jesus had been laid. Azeal remained unseen so that he would not frighten the women. He watched as they walked hand in hand, clinging to each other for strength, singing songs of praise they had learned from Jesus. Tears streamed down their cheeks, and they stopped every so often to bolster each other's courage and ready themselves to face the sealed tomb, a symbol of their dead dreams. Azeal felt a catch in his heart as he observed their pain. *Oh, how they loved their Lord,* he thought.

Along the way, Azeal noticed angels of darkness everywhere. When they saw him, they hurled snarling taunts at him, but he said nothing in response. Instead, he moved closer to the women and spread his mighty wings around them to protect them from attack. Suddenly and without warning, the earth began to shake, and the horde of dark angels began to wail and scream. The women fell to their knees in terror, and Azeal covered them to keep them safe. As Azeal rose, he saw that all the angels of evil had fled. The women looked at each other, stunned, and asked simultaneously, "What was that?"

Shaken, they quickened their pace. As they approached the tomb, they saw that the stone had been rolled away. An angel of God sat upon it. The guards, thoroughly frightened, lay as still as dead men. The two Marys clung to each other in fear. Suddenly, Azeal appeared to them. But he said, "Do not be afraid, for I know that you are looking for Jesus, who was crucified. He is not here; he has risen, just as he said." Azeal's voice was so calm and soothing, and his face glowed with joy; the women knew they had no reason to be afraid. He moved behind them and placed his strong arms around their shoulders and said, "Come and see the place where he lay. Then go quickly and tell his disciples: 'He has risen from the dead and is going ahead of you into Galilee. There you will see him.' Now I have told you."

Amazed, the women hurried away as Azeal had directed. Just a few yards from the tomb, the Savior himself appeared to them. "Greetings," Jesus said. Both women fell to the ground, grabbed hold of his feet, and worshiped him. Azeal knelt directly behind them. Jesus said to the women, "Do not be afraid. Go and tell my brothers to go to Galilee; there they will see me."

As the women, now full of joy, danced toward the city, Jesus smiled approvingly at Azeal and sighed, "Oh, how I love my people." And Azeal answered, "And how they love you, my Lord."

Scriptural Account

After the Sabbath, at dawn on the first day of the week, Mary Magdalene and the other Mary went to look at the tomb.

There was a violent earthquake, for an angel of the Lord came down from heaven and, going to the tomb, rolled back the stone and sat on it. His appearance was like lightning, and his clothes were white as snow. The guards were so afraid of him that they shook and became like dead men.

The angel said to the women, "Do not be afraid, for I know that you are looking for Jesus, who was crucified. He is not here; he has risen, just as he said. Come and see the place where he lay. Then go quickly and tell his disciples: 'He has risen from the dead and is going ahead of you into Galilee. There you will see him.' Now I have told you."

So the women hurried away from the tomb, afraid yet filled with joy, and ran to tell his disciples. Suddenly Jesus met them. "Greetings," he said. They came to him, clasped his feet and worshiped him. Then Jesus said to them, "Do not be afraid. Go and tell my brothers to go to Galilee; there they will see me."

—Matthew 28:1–10

(see also Luke 24:1–10)

Moments I have felt heaven's tender embrace . . .

_____

_____

_____

_____

_____

_____

_____

_____

_____

_____

_____

_____

_____

_____

*You can trust me with all of your cares and burdens because
I deeply care for you.*

—from 1 Peter 5:7

_____

_____

_____

_____

_____

_____

_____

_____

_____

_____

_____

_____

_____

_____

You can count on me to save you from the enemy's snares and harassment. My faithfulness will be your shield.

—from Psalm 91:3–4

So when they met togeth
you at this time going
Israel?" He said to the
the times or dates the
authority. But you wi
Holy Spirit comes on y
nesses in Jerusalem, and
and to the ends of the eart
taken up before their ve
from their sight. They u
the sky as he was goin
dressed in white stood be
they said, "why do you
sky? This same Jesus, i
into heaven, will come ba

six

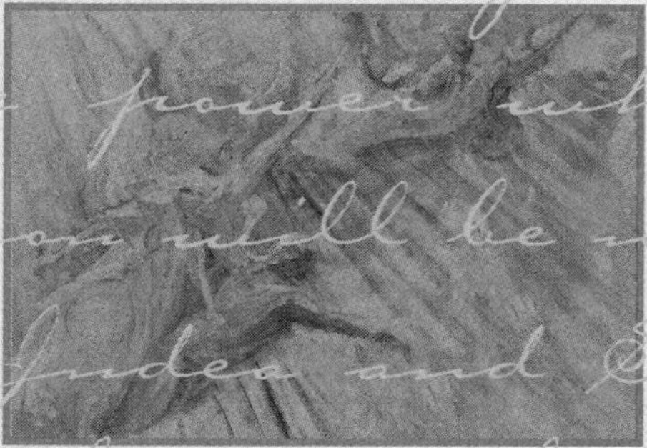

Messengers of Hope

I've set eternity in your heart. The things you see now are only temporary; it's the things you can't see that will last forever. No eye has seen, no ear has heard, no mind has ever conceived all of the awesome and unbelievable things I've prepared for those who love me. The much awaited time of no more tears and no more sorrows is just a moment and a twinkling of an eye away. Feeling homesick yet? Jesus is preparing your place.

Eternally, Your Heavenly Father
—from Ecclesiastes 3:11; 2 Corinthians 2:9, 4:18;
John 14:2; 1 Corinthians 15:51–52

M

Make yourself familiar with the angels and behold them frequently in spirit; for without being seen, they are present with you.

—St. Francis DeSales

Inspirational

Have you noticed that most people avoid saying "Good-bye"? Usually they prefer "See you later" or "See ya" or just "Later." Good-byes are hard to say and even harder to hear. Who doesn't remember a poignant tearful farewell to cherished colleagues, treasured friends, precious parents, or valued neighbors? We don't enjoy the pain of final good-byes.

We like a little hope attached to our departures; we like to believe that we will see that special someone again. There is a permanence to the word good-bye that we would rather not think about—but there doesn't have to be. Even though we know that someday, sometime, somewhere we will have to say good-bye to someone, it doesn't have to be forever. There is One who has challenged the everlasting nature of good-bye. He appeared on the other side of death and said, "I will come back for you." He even sent angelic messengers of hope to affirm the sacred covenant. He broke the restraint of the grave that enslaves

Message

humankind to this world and said, "You will be with me where I am."

Jesus' extraordinary promise of return has caused a thunderous echo of hope to ring in countless hearts for more than two thousand years. Hope for families who have been separated by too much distance and too few resources. Hope for friendships that were set for a lifetime when one of the lives ended abruptly. Hope for parents who had to say unexpected good-byes to children taken by a destructive disease or a tragic accident. Hope for husbands and wives whose lifelong partners' physical hearts stopped while their spiritual love continued to beat strong.

As you experience the uncertainty of everyday existence, don't forget to keep an eye on the heavens. That's where he will appear. His resurrection marked the end to final farewells, his return will mark the end of good-byes forever, and his gathering of God's children will give birth to an eternal chorus of hellos.

He'll Come Again

The morning was rich with sunlight and summer heat as the apostles gathered on the eastern slope of the Mount of Olives. It had been forty days since Christ had come out of the tomb and shown himself to the disciples. Gone from the apostles' thoughts were the bitter images of the crucifixion—the murderous insults hurled by the spitting crowds, the severe beating that staggered the Savior's steady march to the cross, the crown of thorns that mocked his royalty. These could find no suitable housing in the hearts and minds of the disciples who were filled with joy in the presence of their Lord.

Peter's denial of Christ had been transformed from a flaming fire of guilt into a glowing ember by Christ's tender confrontation. Peter felt restored in every way. Though Satan would use the denial to accuse Peter in the future, Christ's love would extinguish the fear and doubt. The desertion of the chosen ones at the arrest scene in the garden and Thomas's post-resurrection disbelief had become distant memories. Christ had embraced each one at some point in his precious time with them and told them they were forgiven. There was no room for the heavy weight of guilt in the future Christ had planned for them. The apostles would need to be focused and free of encumbrances in order to accomplish their mission to share the Good News of Christ with the world.

Each day the apostles had spent with Christ since the resurrection overflowed with building hope and swelling courage. However, in a sad and serious way, these last few days had been different from all the other days they had spent with the Savior. Final words had been spoken. Warnings had been issued. Jesus' instructions had been explicit and exact. Just yesterday, as the eleven met with him, he had stood before each one, placed his hands on their shoulders, looked into their faces, and spoken from his heart: "Peter, stay strong in your convictions and never look back. Pain will accompany you in this life, but peace will ultimately reign." With tears in his eyes he had said, "John, my beloved, our friendship is a treasure for your heart. I will eagerly await our reunion." He had continued down the line of tear-stained faces until he had spoken a special blessing to each one.

The dreaded good-bye hung in the air, but none of them wanted to hear it, especially not from the mouth of the One they had hoped would stay forever. So when they met together, John asked him, "Lord, are you going to restore the kingdom to Israel at this time?" The question was laced with hope. They all hungered for him to answer, "Yes, I am going to stay and rule here on earth," or "Yes, and you will be by my side." But those were not his words. They all sensed that the dreaded farewell was imminent.

He said to them, "It is not for you to know the times or dates the Father has set by his own authority. But you will receive power when the Holy Spirit comes on you; and you will be my witnesses in Jerusalem, and in all Judea and Samaria, and to the ends of the earth."

Then he was taken up before their eyes, and a cloud hid him from their sight. With hands shielding their weeping eyes from the sun, they watched, hoping he would appear one last time.

As they looked intently into the sky, two men dressed in white suddenly stood beside them. One was the angel Oriel, and the other, Stelal. The Father had chosen these particular celestials to be present at this sad scene because of their gifts of encouragement and comfort. He had given them a message of hope for the chosen followers that would take the sting from this painful parting.

Stelal placed his arms around the shoulders of Philip and Thomas; Oriel held the arms of Peter and James. They looked toward heaven with them for a moment, then with broad smiles and warm voices they said, "Men of Galilee, why do you stand here looking at the sky? This same Jesus, who has been taken from you into heaven, will come back in the same way you have seen him go."

The words hit their targets. The hearts of the apostles filled with hope. The tears soon dried and their feet barely touched the ground as they made their way back to town.

The apostles would speak often about the last day

they spent with the Lord of lords. And wherever they shared the news of the ascension, they encouraged the faith of the saints with the message of God delivered by angels: *Jesus will come back in the same way we saw him go into heaven.* And the message always hit home.

It hits the target even now.

Scriptural Account

In my former book, Theophilus, I wrote about all that Jesus began to do and to teach until the day he was taken up to heaven, after giving instructions through the Holy Spirit to the apostles he had chosen. After his suffering, he showed himself to these men and gave many convincing proofs that he was alive. He appeared to them over a period of forty days and spoke about the kingdom of God. On one occasion, while he was eating with them, he gave them this command: "Do not leave Jerusalem, but wait for the gift my Father promised, which you have heard me speak about.

For John baptized with water, but in a few days you will be baptized with the Holy Spirit."

So when they met together, they asked him, "Lord, are you at this time going to restore the kingdom to Israel?"

He said to them: "It is not for you to know the times or dates the Father has set by his own authority. But you will receive power when the Holy Spirit comes on you; and you will be my witnesses in Jerusalem, and in all Judea and Samaria, and to the ends of the earth."

After he said this, he was taken up before their very eyes, and a cloud hid him from their sight.

They were looking intently up into the sky as he was going, when suddenly two men dressed in white stood beside them. "Men of Galilee," they said, "why do you stand here looking into the sky? This same Jesus, who has been taken from you into heaven, will come back in the same way you have seen him go into heaven."

—Acts 1:1–11

$\mathcal{M}$oments I have felt heaven's tender embrace . . .

_____

_____

_____

_____

_____

_____

_____

_____

_____

_____

_____

_____

_____

_____

_____

_____

Don't become weary in running the race of life; you will see a pay-off if you don't quit.

—from Galatians 6:9

_____

_____

_____

_____

_____

_____

_____

_____

_____

_____

_____

_____

_____

_____

Set your heart toward heaven and heavenly things instead of focusing on temporary earthly things.

—from Colossians 3:2

Then the angel said to hi[m]
sandals." And Peter did
you and follow me," the an[gel]
him out of the prison, b[ut]
the angel was doing [was]
thought he was seeing a [vision]
and second guards and ca[me to]
the city. It opened for [them]
went through it. When t[hey]
of one street, suddenly th[e]
came to himself and said
doubt that the Lord sent
Herod's clutches and fr[om]
people were anticipating
him, he went to the ho[use]

seven

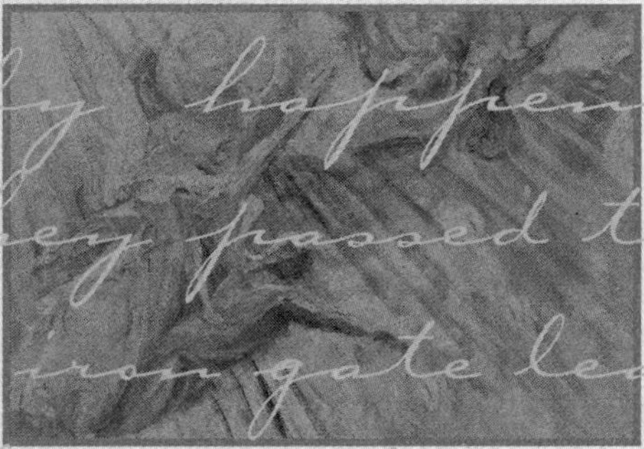

Messengers of Freedom

I have given you the keys to the kingdom of heaven. In me and through faith in me, you can approach God with freedom and confidence. The prayers of the righteous are powerful and effective for day-to-day living. Every time two or more of you gather together in my name, you'll find that I'm right there with you.

Your Prince of Peace,
Jesus

—from Matthew 16:19; Ephesians 3:12; James 5:16;
Matthew 18:19–20

Christians should never fail to sense the operation of an angelic glory. It forever eclipses the world's powers, as the sun does a candle's light.

—Billy Graham

Inspirational

Keys are amazing things, aren't they? Already today, you have probably used keys to open a door, start a car, or lock something of value away. What pocket or purse doesn't jingle with the familiar sound of metal keys colliding in rhythm to each step? Who hasn't felt the panic of realizing that keys have been misplaced? Without keys, much of what we value would remain on the other side of a locked door; so near, yet out of reach forever.

You possess one particular key that performs the unexplainable, the unimaginable, even the miraculous. It unlocks prison doors, opens closed hearts, frees frozen relationships, and protects priceless souls. It is not fashioned from metal, plastic, aluminum, or wood; rather its power is rooted in eternity, and it is activated by your faith. *That key is prayer.*

Use it, and use it often. It won't wear out; in fact,

Message

it becomes stronger each time you insert it into a lock. Use it to escape the prison cell of worry or fear. Turn it to release imprisoned love for God and others. Unlock relationships that have become cold and constricted. Release the protective power of the Almighty God.

Pray, and watch the shackles of sin fall away. Pray, and find fear replaced by peace. Pray, and discover union with the Creator of all. Lift your heart in times of celebration and release thankful joy. Enter the throne room of the heavenly Father and find the door to his heart standing wide open. Come by yourself or with family and friends. Don't let the dust of neglect collect on your key to freedom.

The world may attempt to imprison you with pain and confusion, but you need not be bound. Open your heart, lift your head, and turn the key.

The gloom of the moonless night reflected the hearts and spirits of the people of Jerusalem, especially Jesus' disciples. The events of the previous days, orchestrated by an increasingly bloodthirsty King Herod, had produced a raw tension in the church. The horrific sound of the blade cutting through the neck of James, beloved brother of John, still echoed in the ears of saints across the city. The morbid pleasure this execution brought to many Jews incited Herod to pursue and punish Peter.

Every believer who had witnessed Peter's arrest at the temple spent the afternoon spreading the chilling details about the heavily armed soldiers who harshly escorted Peter to prison. They also told of Peter's instructions to those around him while being led away, "Whatever happens, fear not; God is with us."

In homes throughout Jerusalem, believers gathered to mount a prayer vigil. They petitioned the Father to act quickly to free the apostle who had helped so many others find freedom in Christ. Some prayed boldly in thundering voices, others trembled with timidity, but all were urgent in their pleas, begging God to intercede.

Heaven heard. A call went out to the angel Aphesis. As always, when an urgent need for deliverance from danger arose, Aphesis was the first to be summoned.

His superb strength could break a thousand chains, and no angel could move undetected through the forces of evil as well as he. He had shut the mouths of lions when Daniel was thrown into their den, and he was there when Gideon had led the three hundred against the threat of the Midianites. His radiance was breathtaking, his sparkling eyes intense and alert, his heart loyal to the Father. He hated the schemes and conspiracies of Satan with every fiber of his being.

The archangel Michael found Aphesis at the gates of the throne room. "Aphesis," Michael said, "the prayers of thousands of God's children have reached the Father. He is aware of their heartache and wants them to know that he loves them and is attentive to their requests. Go quickly; Peter is in prison. He has accepted his imminent death, and he is not afraid. Release him and deliver him from the plans of the evil one so that God's children will be assured in their faith. But move carefully. Satan wishes to destroy

Peter. He believes that by doing so, he can defeat the church here and now. We must remind him that nothing will defeat what the Father has begun in his beloved children."

Swiftly, unseen, Aphesis made his way to Israel. As he passed Herod's palace, he was stunned by the number of angels of darkness he saw there. They guarded the doors and perimeter of the palace against any effort by the Father to rescue Herod from his hardened heart. Aphesis thought to himself, *If the Almighty would give the order, I would speed past you and into the presence of Herod before you could recite one more of your deceptions.* But that was not his mission today.

Aphesis reached the prison that held Peter and moved quickly into his cell. He smiled in amusement when he saw how the soldiers had attempted to insure Peter's captivity—by binding him with chains and surrounding him with soldiers, even as he slept. "You will have to do better than that to keep a child of God in prison," he said as he moved toward the sleeping figures. Amazed by how soundly Peter slept, Aphesis thought to himself, *Only a disciple of the Lord could sleep like this in prison while facing death.* He then struck Peter on the side to wake him. "Quick, get up!" he said, and the chains instantly fell from Peter's wrists. Then Aphesis said to him, "Put on your clothes and sandals. Wrap your cloak around you and follow me."

Peter followed Aphesis out of the prison but had no idea that what was happening was real; he thought he was seeing a vision. They passed the first and second guards and came to the iron gate leading into the city. The heavy gate creaked and groaned as Aphesis powered it open. They walked through together and remained silent for the length of one street. Then, sure that he had accomplished his mission, Aphesis suddenly left.

Peter came to himself and said, "Now I know without a doubt that the Lord sent his angel and rescued me from Herod's clutches and from everything the Jewish people were anticipating."

Peter hurried to the house of Mary the mother of John, where many people had gathered to pray. When Peter knocked at the outer entrance, a servant girl, who had been praying earnestly with the rest of the gathered disciples, came to the door. She recognized Peter's voice and was so excited that she ran back without opening the door. "Peter is at the door!" she exclaimed. But no one would believe her. When they finally opened the door and saw him, they were astonished.

Peter motioned for them to be quiet, and he described how the Lord had sent an angel to bring him out of prison. "The Lord heard your prayer for my deliverance, and he has provided. He has once more revealed that he loves us and is attentive to our prayers. Tell James and the brothers all that has happened." In leaving, he said, "Remember my words: Whatever happens, fear not; God is with us."

Back in heaven, when Aphesis reported the rescue of Peter, Michael embraced him and said, "Well done, faithful Aphesis." Aphesis then returned to his post and awaited his next call from the Father to rescue a suffering saint or deliver a child from danger.

He waits and watches even now.

Scriptural Account

It was about this time that King Herod arrested some who belonged to the church, intending to persecute them. He had James, the brother of John, put to death with the sword. When he saw that this pleased the Jews, he proceeded to seize Peter also. This happened during the Feast of Unleavened Bread. After arresting him, he put him in prison, handing him over to be guarded by four squads of four soldiers each. Herod intended to bring him out for public trial after the Passover.

So Peter was kept in prison, but the church was earnestly praying to God for him.

The night before Herod was to bring him to trial, Peter was sleeping between two soldiers, bound with two chains, and sentries stood guard at the entrance. Suddenly an angel of the Lord appeared and a light shone in the cell. He struck Peter on the side and woke him up. "Quick, get up!" he said, and the chains fell off Peter's wrists.

Then the angel said to him, "Put on your clothes and sandals." And Peter did so. "Wrap your cloak around you and follow me," the angel told him. Peter followed him out of the prison, but he had no idea that what the angel was doing was really happening; he thought he was seeing a vision. They passed the first and second guards and came to the iron gate leading to the city. It opened for them by itself, and they went through it. When they had walked the length of one street, suddenly the angel left him.

Then Peter came to himself and said, "Now I know without a doubt that the Lord sent his angel and rescued me from Herod's clutches and from everything the Jewish people were anticipating."

When this had dawned on him, he went to the house of Mary the mother of John, also called Mark, where many people had gathered and were praying. Peter knocked at the outer entrance, and a servant girl named Rhoda came to answer the door. When she recognized Peter's voice, she was so overjoyed she ran back without opening it and exclaimed, "Peter is at the door!" "You're out of your mind," they told her. When she kept insisting that it was so, they said, "It must be his angel." But Peter kept on knocking, and when they opened the door and saw him, they were astonished. Peter motioned with his hand for them to be quiet and described how the Lord had brought him out of prison. "Tell James and the brothers about this," he said, and then he left for another place.

—Acts 12:1–17

Moments I have felt heaven's tender embrace . . .

_____

_____

_____

_____

_____

_____

_____

_____

_____

_____

_____

_____

_____

_____

My eyes are on you, and my ears are attentive to your cry.
The prayers of the righteous are powerful and effective.

—from Psalm 34:15; James 5:16

_____

_____

_____

_____

_____

_____

_____

_____

_____

_____

_____

_____

_____

For where two or more of you are gathered in my Son's name, Jesus is right there with you.

—from Matthew 18:20

_____
_____
_____
_____
_____
_____
_____
_____
_____
_____
_____
_____
_____
_____
_____

Things that seem impossible to you aren't even a challenge for me.

—from Mark 10:27